DIASPORA OF THINGS

poems by

Jill Pearlman

Finishing Line Press
Georgetown, Kentucky

DIASPORA OF THINGS

Copyright © 2025 by Jill Pearlman
ISBN 979-8-89990-096-9 First Edition
All rights reserved under International and Pan-American Copyright Conventions. No part of this book may be reproduced in any manner whatsoever without written permission from the publisher, except in the case of brief quotations embodied in critical articles and reviews.

ACKNOWLEDGMENTS

To my dear friends and family, deep gratitude for your support over the years. And my heartfelt thanks to my editor, Christen Kincaid, and publisher, Leah Huete de Maines, of Finishing Line Press for guiding this personal work into print.

Publisher: Leah Huete de Maines
Editor: Christen Kincaid
Cover Art and Design: Raina Wellman
Author Photo: George Lange

Order online: www.finishinglinepress.com
also available on amazon.com

Author inquiries and mail orders:
Finishing Line Press
PO Box 1626
Georgetown, Kentucky 40324
USA

For my mother, Doris Medvene Pearlman

*Studying the beautiful is a duel
where the artist cries out in fright
before suffering defeat.*

—Charles Baudelaire

*If you won—you are dead and I
am dead, in my way, why are we
standing here sharing this fabric,
this flesh, this tissue?*

*You double agent,
you believed too*

*We are world within worlds,
my need tucked inside yours
or mirrored; rather than
diminishing me, perhaps kin*

This is the amber cocoon she created
for herself—for others—
not a sharp edge in the place.

Outside, music of leaves, a thick symphony.

Gold-green light skitters through palms
in the middle distance.
Light is housed as ripples of silk.

A limestone villa, a palace of protection
for her sphinxness,
my mother used her tongue like a knife.

After the shipwreck, the curious scour
mute and restless items for clues.
Things are now awake, at full attention,
freed from the daze of possession—

lit lit lit as captives coming
to their own bright selves
as sleepwalkers coming
to their own loud shine

part of the warp and weave,
tissue of falling and becoming,

voiced in my ear's fabric
the long-denied-speak.
Crystal birdspeak. Leopard stoolspeak.
Jade flower bouquet speak.
Stained old potspeak. Converted
Greek jarspeak. Hairbrushspeak.
Address book speak.

The soft pencil of our life together.
The warehouse of your mind. The tissue
of our flesh and fingers.   Speak.

She was a redhead. A red flame needs a soft protected bed.

The arch of an eyebrow in the mirror. Auburn.

Born ten days after Elizabeth Taylor.

A line she uttered once, no more, after her design work was done:

"I've gone to a better place. It just happens to be here!"

Bees in the corridor
of my death,
practice, practice
in the antechamber,
the prelude room.

All hail to the buzz
of what we do
to no longer be.

My hours of witness
speed my witness of minutes

though every day
I practice
is another day
still living.

In this mood, I could
write an ode
to a chamber pot.

Could I sing a low dirge
to green spotlights
in the earth
that tickle leaves?
To fluff on a puddle's
wrinkled surface,
to painted monkeys who sit
in tidy waistcoats
cross-legged, perplexed,
what can be said about the grief
of those sad, elegant creatures?

Remembering and forgetting
and remembering:
Even the dust sings in its corners.

Sitting by the pool, a few gulls overhead.
There is only pouring. There is only emptying.
The humid air keeps refilling itself. It is paddled
by palms: palm leaves do the oaring.

Double glass doors—a threshold for
mutual viewings.

The silvered lamp
with its beaded shade
and many eyes of glass.
An undercover agent or spy,
an observant child.
The lids of my pores blink back.
It lays its hands on me, palpitating.

The varnish of a table glows
with the touch of curious fingers.
That chair! Its feet, its vacant lap.
It lives as a sitting body, a relative
once removed.

The strolling wired sculpture:
how thin our fate, thin thread—
lacquering our sadness
with elegance.

Birds fly in a fast-moving shadow
pulling words across the page
as I am reading.

In the distance, how many shards of light,

    of color reflected back at me—

        to change the nature of my eye.

Stacks and stacks of napkins—so beautifully ironed,
the creases would break your heart.
She didn't even cook. She entertained—maybe
herself. Phoo to cooking!
She kept *I Hate to Cook Book* on her shelf,
along with the bitter joys of Betty Friedan
and winkaholic Andy Warhol.
Let them eat their hearts out:
her leather jacket better than a tired apron.

Later, once we kids were gone,
I'd pull down the door of the General Electric
in her new apartment to find
twelve-pack cans of Coca-Cola
stored in the oven.

"To heck with the domestic! Down with dishes.
Two girl friends are dying (getting old is not for babies).
What I wouldn't give for a slice
of chocolate cake!"

The wind polishes
the glass. A mirrored bar, the kind
they had in the Depression, when Hollywood
made films to make everyone forget
the Depression (as parents stuck their children
in the orphanage and years later hoisted them out).

Sweeping along marble floors
in a white apartment, Joan Crawford's invisible
silk angels rustling the hem, offering her lover
a cocktail with linen napkin. From the stacks
of napkins, mother must have imagined forty lovers.

The rattle of rain
on high palm leaves
thin like my skin
grief though old
thrown against
tissue of your self
so woven
in this house
still warm
we are unthreading
flaying, every strike
against beauty
hits me
as transgression

How long
it took me to sit,
to see the shimmer
from pain to beauty
and back
feel the unsaid
(the less said, more felt)

I could always read
a forest or pond, I had
to wait to touch
your lacerations
close, closer to that
mystery

the last plane,
the tissue, the thingy flesh
this masterpiece
of our encounter
better than both of us
not ready
for armies
or Salvation

Good God, this was supposed to be fun!

What use is beauty, if weak beauty—none at all!

In her library

Odilon Redon's mystical eye

sees me seeing her
reading this book

she, as a young art student

asking herself what is seeing
or what is it seeing

what is this eye loosely tied to a basket

floating gamely across the sky

The nerve to place the furcula, the wishbone, a forked bone from the neck and the breast of a Thanksgiving bird, in the chandelier above the dining room table

Your chairs have good bones

Look at this fabulous promiscuity. These spotted vases with the Marshall's sticker next to a Frank Stella. Spices from a Turkish bazaar or Lake Worth 99-cent store. The gay wit of bird nests that fit into Norma Shearer's Marie Antoinette wig

Let them speak their magic

Diaspora of things. Professionals
arrive in white pants and loafers,
unpacking their steely eye. Dollar
figures are set/ identities swapped.
Made object again, they are sullen,
not flashing their magic
to the unworthy, they become
cheap commodities.

What of the unloved objects, the orphans?
I want to shepherd them away
from ruin, rain, dumpsters.

The trash is a hungry beast.

How droll, that nothing mattered.
The '60s stewardess carrying a bag labeled Trash:
how sad that she advertises her low self-esteem!

How sharp the wounds must be
to fence so fiercely—

and be betrayed by beauty.

For a day, packs of movers move in.
On their belt loops: roll of cello tape
with first names in magic marker.
Bubble wrap and crates and cardboard.
Unwinding the place bit by bit.
Blisters. All speaking Cuban.
A bleached blond with shaved crown,
a roller blade kid who flashes me a card
to his side hustle, pool cleaning service.
Clatter! An older gent turns a mirrored
table upside down, glass pieces
scatter: everyone groans.

The garish night in the parking lot,
underworld of Walmart.
Bubble wrap central. Babies in arms
or clutching parents' hands, fresh from the 9 to 9.
Feels like a party: tinsel, candles, coals.
Who doesn't own a truck, a tattoo?
Or drink crumbs from a shiny Doritos bag.
The long bony fingers of the cashier,
all the years she'd been banging on those keys.

O sweet burned pot
in your swish kitchen,
gentle pot (perhaps called saucepan)
in '60s succotash tone
that we redeemed for a book
of S&H green stamps
at the supermarket
that replaced the kosher butcher
Federman & Fogel
where rubbery feet of chickens swung
the *yidishe gas* (the Jewish street)
the old-world fruit vendor and Jewish bakeries
that made cookie bows with sprinkles,
cheap food dyes, rye breads,
marble, pumpernickel.

In this wealth and profusion
we use not a whistling kettle,
not an electric kettle,
but that salvaged, six-inch,
green stamps pot with Teflon
on the bottom, a burn mark
from a red-hot electric stove coil.
The rich dine on irony!

How can you separate art and life, and why would you

O morning light on bearded man, on mulberry silk:
how goodly you rake your rice paddy again and again

O pink rosettes of Venetian glass:
Ode me, Italian craftsmen, with your gentle seductions.
May we never scorn adolescent sighs and passions

O sketches of narcissus leaves:
You will be the base of a lamp; how obsessively you trace
 the frail trembling of life, stigmata of beauty!

O seated monk:
You wear around your neck New Year's beads, gentle
mark of time like the rings of the tree from which you hail

O crystal birds on the wall:
How many empty hours we sat together; now finally as I
was looking into them, they gave their truest song

O sewing hand:
Trace of artisans who swore the tassels and borders into being.
Sewed long Italian vowels of elaboration. Giorgio, Alessandra,
Salvatore, your touch is immortal

O mirrored bar:
How elegantly you sit shift in a corner awaiting cocktail hour
 (a breath held in wonder and suspension must be released)

O perfume flask:
I carried from here to there… in your fragrance, I walked
right through the open door to the open air

Put this in larger than a jewelry box: the Lexus. Hard, color facts first. 2006. Blue. Royal. Creamy interior, Alabaster; cold asparagus soup. A throne on wheels. Very grand old dame, stately, like a state, say, Rhode Island or better a tax haven, Andorra. A frou-frou. Little throwaway that crashes in price when you leave the lot, though we wondered if they sprayed new car smell over the years. To feel like a million bucks. To feel born with a silver spoon when you were born, father carrying a pinball machine on his back. Mother a flapper, eloped with father Joe to St. Louis where they owned some sort of dancehall, had to slink home with tail between their legs. Lexus? Love affair with cars. Not like they bought a castle in England. I mean, she dyed her own hair. The cloth with an old diaper pin still on the side of the bathtub. Where did they go in it? I think of a note I scrawled at the bottom of her inventory: Jillie, if I'd spent my money on art instead of jewelry, what masterpieces would I have? But I wouldn't have had so much fun.

I am one pole to
the other; I and I

One says my dark—my liqueur—
is not your dark.
If mine is wondrous, why should I drink your bitter cup?

One wants hard proof.
She uses it to maneuver.

One looks strangers in the eye, smiles;
One has been cheated too many times.

One heard a word fall soft in the forest's liquid,
like a god undoing his form.

One likes her animals in aspic. Or ceramic.
Humans often included.

One will not wash in a shared hotel tub.
She is tough as nails, and never gets them manicured.

One keeps the door open for fugitive desires.
Someone's hand always in a door. Swollen knuckles. Always a door.

I see grass, fresh and green,
in handfuls
yanked up
clumps
its naked roots

Then hair silken, blond,
as a summer corn

Around its ear
torn from its place

Behind your ear, a plan;
a dirge, a new song, roots of inertia
scoured, roots tickled, replanted

Oh grass; when elephants fight,
the grass suffers

Flâneur. With a crystal glass
of Armagnac,
in a green gleam of
absinthe hours, I wandered—

caught by moonshine on the etch
of palmettos in the hallway

things calling
through the thin glass of self.

Tassels in their bright skirts
sconces and their courtesan hips

the sinuous curve of a table leg
a bruising of gold leaf

each tableau in the moonlight
slumbers on the velvet of our misery.

And aftershock:
a chair plucks its liquid guitar strings
palms shed great sheaths of body trunks

strewing long tracks of desire
and extravagance

I can't control what comes in;
beauty, or monsters, the sea
teems with them.

How can a body rise up
and rinse its face from the tap,
keep tap tap tapping,
drink water even if it's bottled?
Behind the consoles, in the waters,
invitation to the depths, the immensity.
The documents alone will sink you.
The undersigned hereby informs you.
Acute awareness of the individual's
plight and nature. The thinnest
thread that we cling to.
To be signed and dated by you.
Remit to Dr. Myra Bone
for chief complaint: osteoporosis.
Southern Building Inspection,
6169 Gun Club Road.
The house has good bones.
And mold.
Furnished: Heavily.
Weather: 79 degrees, humidity, 63 percent.
Previous Day: Same.
The suffering of someone who stuffs down
her suffering. How sharp that knife.
Exquisite understanding reduced to a
witness of paper.
Perishability becomes a hardened thing.
Nothing to fuss about.
It fascinates for what we can't say.

What a riot they once had,
the old gang. Birds of a feather,
in their fine teased toupees
and mother, minus a breast
from her early forties,
in a black-zipped bustier.

Or holding a saucer, an almost careless
swallow; as she spoke, droll, toes
slipping from her sandal, a slant glance
over the room, mixed satisfaction.

All those hard knocks, from a cruel
species. Nothing is given. Women
are smarter but played dumb; everyone has an angle.
Do what must be done. Faint smell of jasmine.

That painted lioness in the corner…
At least she won't claw me
like some other jungle cats!

It would never last forever, friends,
aesthetes, lovers—thus the fury
and abandon. The carousel of men and women
in and out of closets. Doors open/closed.
Masquerade—oh bitter fun.

From hope to bitterness to peace, all under one roof. A life.

How do we iron the napkins
with their pure unwrinkled skin?
Just don't use them.

How have I just understood
the *suffering* in *passion*?

The more suffering, the more com-passion.

Passio the iron over the linens. Could I have come so far,
and still be so far?

Not to see how everything reeks of suffering—plain as the face of day.
In the napkins. In the trembling sketches of the narcissus, all joy and
pain.

I am of everything that isn't me.
And cannot say more, though I

have words, and she had things,
what was meant by those stacks of perfect napkins.

Virgil asks what use is beauty when armies come...
"What can music do against the weapons of soldiers?
When eagles come, tell me what doves can possibly do?"

What had I been thinking, that fangless beauty could survive in this world? Amidst the cravenness?

I can't be wrong there. The wind will not deplete tenderness.

I build with a handful of words
for the sake of an encounter

trying to be delicate, letting the soft parts speak

as you, with your things, left presence
that could carry over

that we might dissolve and resolve and reimagine—

All my failures, I can claim, are human

I've gone backwoods, handy with a rifle. Suspicious of strangers.

I sometimes stand at my own backdoor and raise it suspiciously—hold it to myself.

And who are you, stranger?

Stranger selves.

How to hold self? The holding the point.

Stranger, selves. The ones that disappear and hide behind others.

That we are all one big heart—not just us, but everyone—imagine!

Jill Pearlman's poetry explores ecstasy in the decentered world and decentered self. Originally from Pittsburgh, she has lived in New York, Paris, French Catalonia and Providence, RI. Her poems (The Common, Salamander, Barrow Street, La Piccioletta Barca) wander the world as impatient travelers, reflecting voices of fluidity, phenomena and transcultural values. They draw from various philosophies: phenomenology, Jewish spiritual traditions, French modernism, physical and metaphysical travel, and the spontaneity of direct perception. She has produced multimedia poetry series: "Trees Road Vertigo," documenting the fate of plane trees in France, and "Mirrors, a conversation with Avivah Gottlieb Zornberg." She studied art history, worked as a music and arts journalist in New York and is the mother of two superb daughters. She posts work at jillpearlman.com and on Bluesky.